Joe Pass
on Guitar

Transcriptions by KENN CHIPKIN

Project Manager/Editor: Aaron Stang
Additional Text by Kenn Chipkin
Technical Editor: Albert Nigro
Engraver: Andrew Gregor
Front Cover Photo: Margaret Ford
Art Layout: Joann Carrera

Contents

Blues Intro

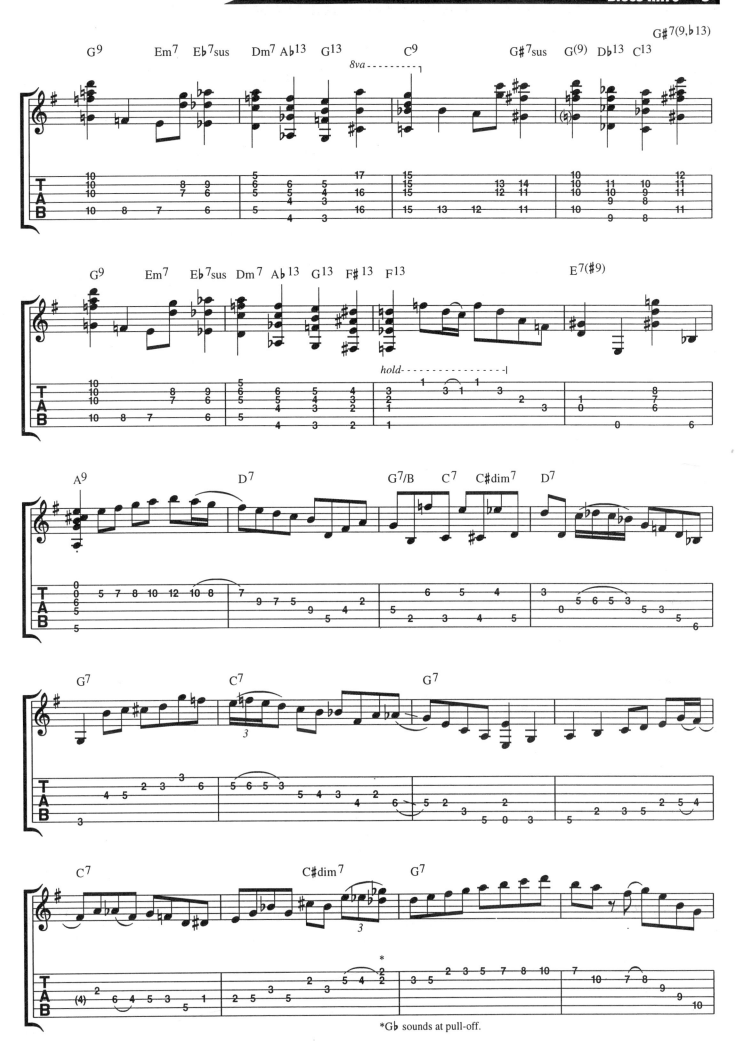

*Gb sounds at pull-off.

*A sounds at pull-off.

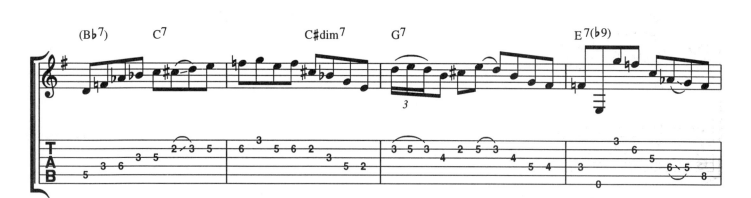

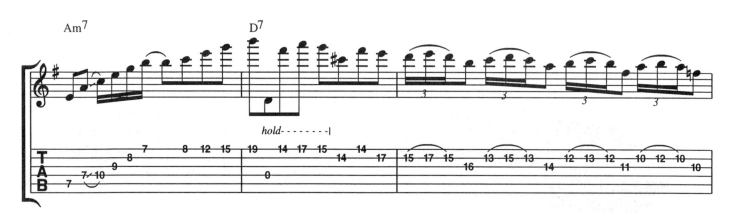

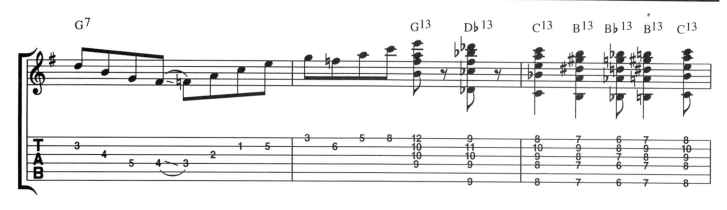

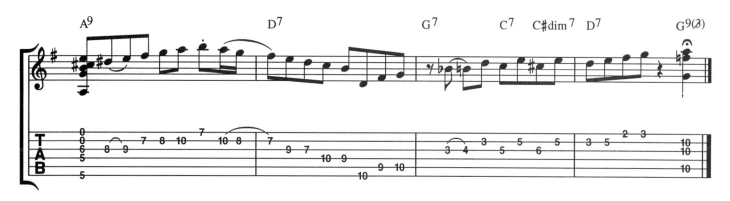

CAGED

The acronym "CAGED" stands for the roots of the basic open position major chords: C, A, G, E and D. You can re-finger these forms so that your index finger acts as the nut, converting each to a barre chord that can be used all over the neck. First, play the basic open chords with the given fingering, and then lay your index finger over the nut and re-finger accordingly.

Example 1 (CD 3)

Five Folk/Country Chords:

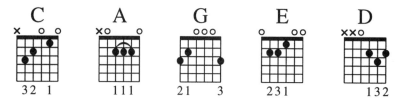

Example 2 (CD 4)

From the five folk chords we can derive five different fingerings and positions for a C chord. All five are root position chords (C in bass).

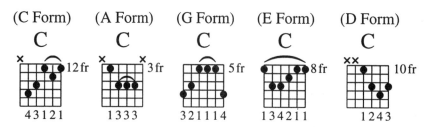

Example 3 (CD 5)

It is very useful to be able to play all 12 major chords within a given area of the neck, and this example illustrates how to do so in three neck areas. The roots of the chords are derived from a cycle of 4ths. A 1st inversion chord form (3rd in bass) is used in order to keep all the chord fingerings in close proximity.

1st Inversion Form

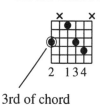

3rd of chord

Once you are comfortable with these forms, change the qualities to minor and dominant. Next, include 7ths, 9ths and other tensions, as the original major types are the building blocks of your fretboard access.

Area 1:

C	F	Bb	Eb	Ab	Db/C#

3 2 1 1 1 4	4 3 1 2 1	1 3 4 2 1 1	1 3 3 3	1 2 4 3	3 2 1 1 1 4

F#	B	E	A	D	G
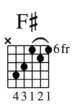		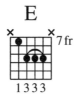			
4 3 1 2 1	1 3 4 2 1 1	1 3 3 3	1 3 4 2 1 1	1 3 3 3	2 1 3 4

Area 2:

C	F	Bb	Eb	Ab	Db/C#
					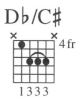
1 3 3 3	2 1 3 4	3 2 1 1 1 4	4 3 1 2 1	1 3 4 2 1 1	1 3 3 3

F#	B	E	A	D	G
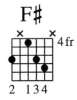			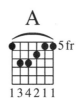		
2 1 3 4	3 2 1 1 1 4	4 3 1 2 1	1 3 4 2 1 1	1 3 3 3	1 3 4 2 1 1

Area 3:

C	F	Bb	Eb	Ab	Db/C#
	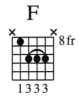			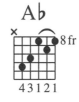	
1 3 4 2 1 1	1 3 3 3	2 1 3 4	3 2 1 1 1 4	4 3 1 2 1	1 3 4 2 1 1

F#	B	E	A	D	G
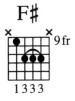	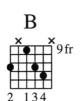	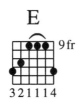	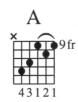	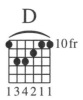	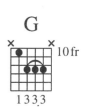
1 3 3 3	2 1 3 4	3 2 1 1 1 4	4 3 1 2 1	1 3 4 2 1 1	1 3 3 3

Right-Hand Technique

CD 6

FINGERSTYLE

It is important to develop the ability to play fingerstyle, where you can choose any combination of notes from a given chord. Playing with a pick does not afford you this flexibility. Unlike the standard classical approach of assigning specific fingers to the six strings, you should seek to find the finger/string relationships that are most comfortable for you. No particular system is necessary. The choices you make can be as free and improvised as the style of jazz itself.

USING A PICK

A small pick is recommended to keep the closest proximity to the strings as possible. This will help you to "feel" the instrument more than if a regular (or large-size) pick were used. In general, use alternate picking when on a single string. When changing from one string to another in either direction, use a downstroke, despite that it may break the pattern of alternate picking. Downstrokes tend to give definition to your string attack.

Example 4 (CD 7)

This illustrates a typical alternate picking approach. All changes from string to string employ the downpick exclusively. Joe seldom uses "backpicking" (or up-picked notes) when descending from high to low strings.

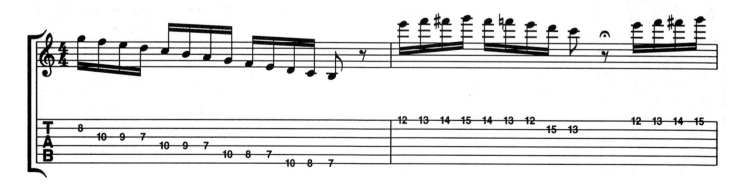

Example 5 (CD 8)

More of the same picking approach is shown here with lines based on G7. We will look at dominant chord improvisation more closely later on in the book.

Left-Hand Technique

Pull-offs, Hammer-ons and Slides

Guitar players use these slurring techniques to create a more lyrical, legato sound than continuous alternate picking can offer. By playing multiple notes with a single pick attack, the phrasing begins to imitate a singer, where many notes can be heard within a single word or syllable.

Example 6 (CD 9 & 10)

In this example there are several different combinations of pull-offs, hammer-ons and slides that can be isolated for practice purposes. (The fragments transcribed here do not include the repetitions as played on the recording.) At this time, it is not essential to understand the harmonic implications of the lines. Simply practice the fragments until they are under control. It would be a worthy time investment to transpose the musical ideas to the lower strings, as they will feel slightly more difficult to produce due to string mass.

Example 6A:

Example 6B:

This line highlights a hammer-on to a new string; a technique that allows great mobility and agile, legato playing. Another goal of this approach is to strengthen the third finger.

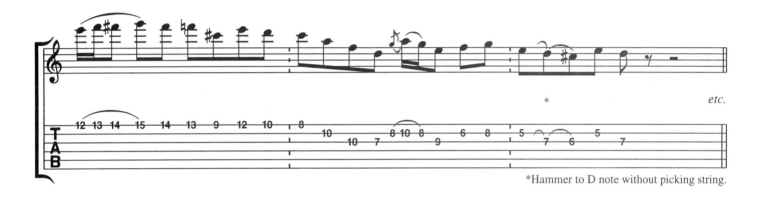

*Hammer to D note without picking string.

Harmonic Families: Maj7, Dom7, Min7

CD (11)

To free yourself of complexity and "over thinking" when soloing, it is best to boil chords down to the most basic terms possible. Instead of concerning yourself with every extension (9, 11, 13) or tension tone (#5/b5,#9/b9, etc.) present in a given chord, perceive that chord as belonging to one of three "families." These three families are major 7, dominant 7 and minor 7. Their intervallic structures are as follows:

	TRIAD			7th	Example in C:			
Maj7:	1	3	5	7	Cmaj7: C	E	G	B
Dom7:	1	3	5	b7	C7: C	E	G	Bb
Min7:	1	b3	5	b7	Cm7: C	Eb	G	Bb

Note that the maj7 and dom7 families are based on a major triad with two different 7ths (b7 and b7 respectively) while the min7 family is based on a minor triad with a b7.

Diminished 7 and Augmented Subfamilies

The dim7 and augmented chords can be considered "subfamilies" of the dom7. Although these chords are commonly used entities unto themselves, in a jazz context they are viewed as "substitutions" where dim7 becomes a dom7(b9) sound, and augmented becomes a dom7(#5) sound.

Diminished 7 Chord: 1 b3 b5 bb7
  Ex: Cdim7 = C Eb Gb Bbb

This is a minor triad with a lowered 5th degree and a double-lowered 7th degree.

Augmented 7 Chord: 1 3 #5
  Ex: Caug7 = C E G#

This is a dominant 7th chord with a raised 5th degree.

Since all the notes in a diminished 7th chord are equal, in respect to chord substitution, any one of the notes in the dim7 shape can be considered the 3, 5, b7 or b9 of a dominant 7 chord.

Diminished 7 Chord Substitution Process
Ex: C♯dim7 as substitute for A7

STEP 1   Spell Dim7 sound: (consecutive minor 3rds)

C♯   E   G   B♭
1   ♭3   ♭5   ♭♭7

STEP 2   Relate chord intervalically to A7:

A7:

A   C♯   E   G
1   3   5   ♭7

C♯dim 7:

C♯   E   G   B♭
3   5   ♭7   ♭9

STEP 3   Revoice notes to form "guitaristic" shape that symmetrically divides the
neck into four equal parts, with its inversions:

C♯dim7(A7♭9)   Edim7(A7♭9)   Gdim7(A7♭9)   B♭dim7(A7♭9)

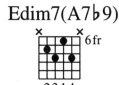
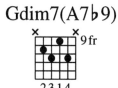
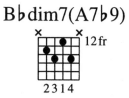

In Step 1, we see that the dim7 sound is constructed by "stacking" consecutive minor 3rds which
divides the octave into four equal parts. In Step 2, the dim7 chord is analyzed in the context of the
dom7 family (A7). The intervals present will always be 3, 5, ♭7 and ♭9 of the dominant chord.
When we assume any one of these four notes to be a dom7 chord tone, the remaining three notes
complete the 3, 5, ♭7, ♭9 equation (always excluding the root).

Finally, Step 3 revoices the stacked minor 3rds into a commonly used "guitaristic" shape on the top
four strings. This shape inverts itself every three frets as it divides the guitar neck into equal parts -
as shown by the chord frames.

Augmented Chord Substitution Process:

STEP 1   Spell augmented sound: (consecutive major 3rds)

A   C♯   E♯
1   3   ♯5

STEP 2   Voicings are naturally "guitaristic"

A   C♯   E♯

STEP 3   Add the ♭7 (G)

The process concerning the augmented chord is less involved and allows for the root (A) of the substitution chord to be used. In Step 1, the augmented chord is shown to be constructed by stacking consecutive major 3rds, dividing the octave into three equal parts. Step 2 shows the voicing of the augmented sound to possess a naturally "guitaristic" shape that symmetrically divides the neck into three equal parts. Now there is no need to relate the chord to A7 because it is already related by its root and 3rd. In Step 3, we add the b7 (G) to the augmented chord wherever possible to complete the "dom7($\sharp$5) sound."

Harmonic Families: Major 7

With Cmaj7 as our example, we will be stepping directly up the major scale from the root to the major 7th (C D E F G A B), rather than employing arpeggios.

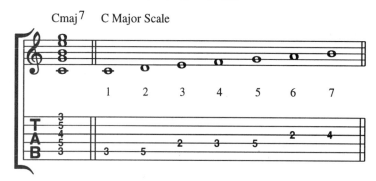

Example 7 (CD 12 - 14)

Here is a spontaneous line based on Cmaj7 that is completely diatonic.

This line is derived from the following harmonization. The harmonization is again fully diatonic, carrying C major scale notes under the melodic line. It is best to think of all the chord shapes as "one big Cmaj7 chord," rather than the separate chords which they may be implying - like Em7 or Am7, for example. Note the variations in 7B as compared to 7A.

Example 7A:

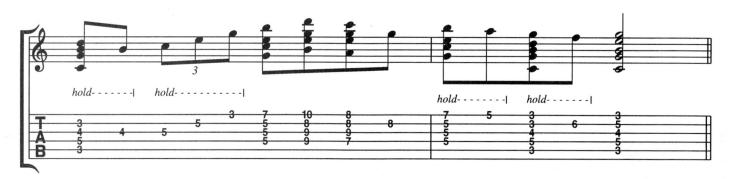

Example 7B:

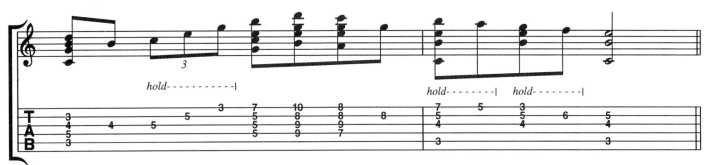

Example 8 (CD 14)

Transposing the melodic idea we are playing to other string groups and neck positions is essential to your musical understanding of this material. A firm grasp on transposing musical information will ultimately improve your musicianship, as you exploit the entire instrument. Make a mental note of the subtle changes in fingering as this line transposes through the different strings and positions.

Example 9 (CD 15)

Unrelated to the last line comes this non-diatonic example. "Gravity" is at play here, as the line falls from the maj7th (B) down to the 5th (G) with chromatic passing tones B♭ and A♭ in two different octaves. From this point on, continue to transpose each new line to other strings and positions as shown in the previous example.

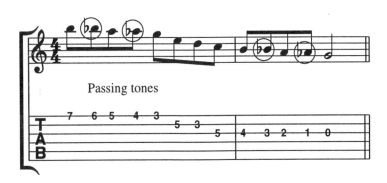

Passing tones

Example 10 (CD 16)

Next are a variety of longer lines that span more than one octave. Pay close attention to how non-diatonic notes are chosen and how they resolve to chord tones.

Example 11 (CD 17)

This line uses a very colorful interval called the #11, which in jazz is a popular tension on a Maj7 chord. For Cmaj7, the #11 is F#, which is found in two octaves here.

Example 12 (CD 18)

The following arpeggio/line superimposes a G triad (beats 1 and 2), and an Em triad on beat 3, ending with a sweet Cmaj9 chord with a high 9th (D) on top in bar 2.

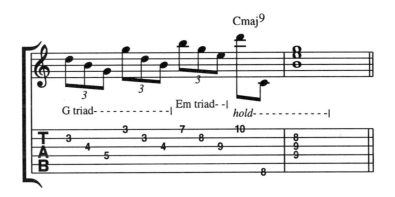

Example 13 (CD 19)

This line has a "falling-down-stairs" quality to it - again due to the "gravity" of the downward chromatic passing tones: Bb and Ab. Once more, pay close attention to where the non-chord tones resolve to chord tones, the rhythmic placement of which can make or break a line.

Example 14 (CD 20)

Here is a phrase built on a diatonic pattern using a C major scale, beginning on a low 5th (G). The pattern is based on the interval of a 2nd, followed by the interval of a 3rd. This relationship continues for six beats and ends in a scalewise descent from the 3rd (E), landing on an A note, which adds up to a C6 chord (bar 3).

Example 15 (CD 21)

The #11 (F#) is highlighted again in this arpeggio/line which suggests Em9 (E G B D F#) in bar 1, and Gmaj7 (G B D F#) in bar 2. Bar 3 creates a structure based mostly on 4ths.

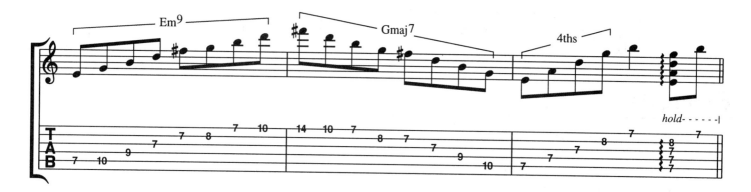

Example 16 (CD 22)

This arpeggio/line is derived from the Cmaj9 chord as shown in the frame below. After reaching the highest note (D), the line shifts out of 2nd position, reaching as high as the 10th fret. This is another idiomatic example of a diatonic line that should be transposed to other positions and other keys as it is a good springboard for single-line soloing on a major 7 chord.

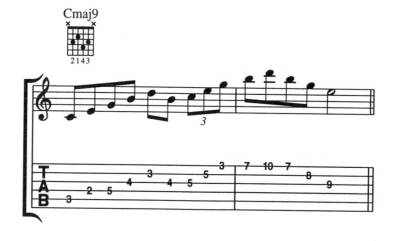

Example 17 (CD 23)

Here is a very strong example of C major scale usage. The line has a definite direction and identity with a variety of intervallic skips between notes. Its most identifiable characteristic is that it begins and ends on the major 3rd (E).

Example 18 (CD 24)

This line hints at superimposing the V7 altered chord (G7alt.), which we will delve deeper into shortly. In this case, the "hint" is the Ab and B within close proximity of each other, suggesting the b9 and major 3rd of G7 (G B D F Ab).

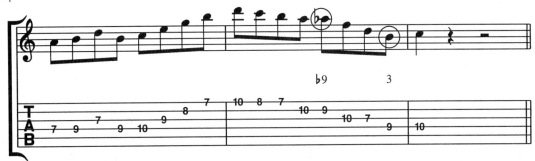

Example 19 (CD 25)

Now the superimposition is further fleshed out with notes that strongly suggest the G7 altered chord. The B and Ab occur more often (and in two octaves) as well as the introduction of the #5 (D#) of G7. From this point on, when non-diatonic notes appear, you may want to consider the possibility of their association with the V7 altered sound. With G7 as the example, the "altered sound" is characterized by the following possibilities:

	1	**3**	**5**	**b7**	**9**	**11**
Diatonic G7:	G	B	D	F	A	C
Altered G7:	G	B	Db/D#	F	Ab/A#	C#
			b5/#5		b9/#9	#11

The color tones (G7 altered) can be superimposed over Cmaj7 for the duration of one bar, finally resolving to a Cmaj7 chord tone. Check out the diagram below.

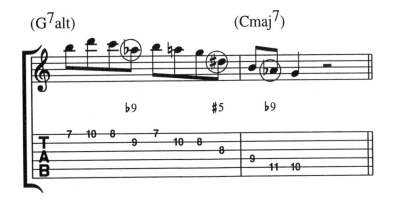

Example 20: Major Etude (CD 26)

This example pulls together all the principles we have been working on thus far and takes a few steps further in this study on improvising over a static maj7 chord. Check out these points of importance for study:

1. Look into the use of pure diatonic lines and what makes them tick. What chord tones do they begin and end on? What is the shape and range of the line? Finally, how is scalewise movement balanced with skips?

2. Pay close attention to non-diatonic notes. Are they used as ascending/descending passing tones? Do they accent a chord-tone only? Or are they used in the context of a substitution of V7 altered over Cmaj7, as discussed? Telltale signs would be the rhythmic placement of the substitution in the bar and especially how the tension is built and released (resolved) to specific chord tones. As you will notice, these lines commonly resolve to the 5th (G) of the Cmaj7 chord.

3. The bracketed or circled notes and phrases will assist you in understanding their harmonic purpose in the line. I stands for Cmaj7, while V7 stands for G7 (altered). For example, "I: 3" refers to E, the 3rd of the Cmaj7 chord, while "V7:♭9" refers to A♭, the ♭9 of the G7 chord.

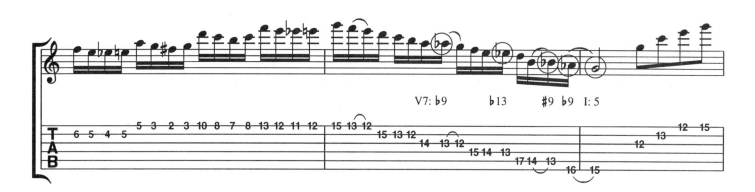

*Non-diatonic.

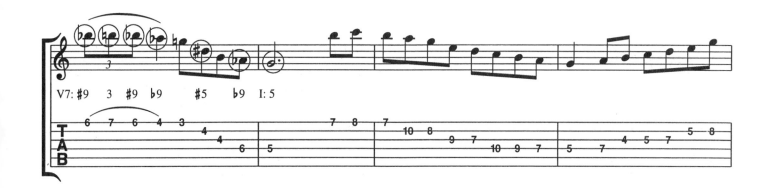

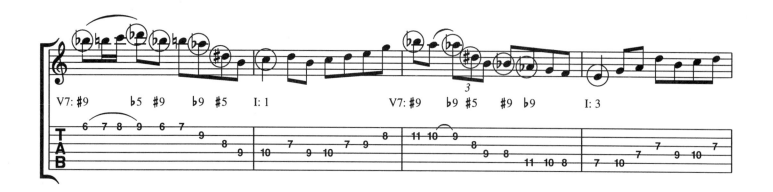

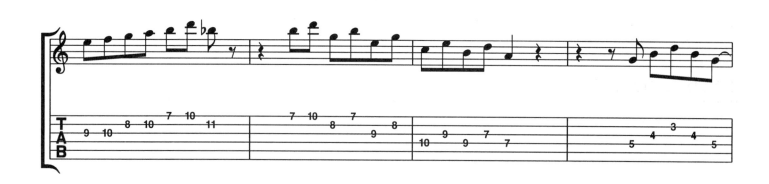

Harmonic Families: Minor 7

As we move on to the minor 7 family, continue to consider simplifying complex chords to free yourself of over thinking while improvising.

Example 21 (CD 27)

First warm up to the sharp contrast in sound and mood that minor chords suggest. Play this 3rd position "grip" of Cm7 and consider what the chord suggests when played linearly.

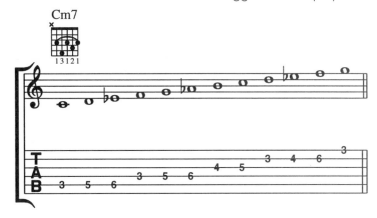

This particular scale is known as **harmonic minor** and its intervallic spelling is: 1 2 ♭3 4 5 ♭6 7. The two other minor scales that are used in this section are **natural minor** (1 2 ♭3 4 5 ♭6 ♭7) and **melodic minor** (1 2 ♭3 4 5 6 7), and we will deal with them as they come up.

Example 22 (CD 28)

This arpeggio/line fills out the Cm7 sound up to the 9th (D), the sum total becoming Cm9 - if played as a "block" chord.

Example 23 (CD 29)

This one uses the same chord tones, only it starts from the ♭3 (E♭) and also throws in the 4th (F) for a bit of tension.

Example 23A:

Example 23B is the same line, only harmonized with notes derived from the melodic minor scale.

Example 23B:

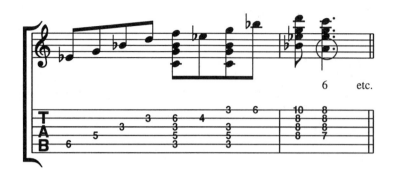

Example 24 (CD 30)

This line makes use of downward chromatic passing tones that surround the Cm7 barre form. Chord tones are circled. The idea ends on the 5th (G) of the Cm7 chord, as it is surrounded by upper and lower neighbor tones - Ab and F#. This "surrounding-of-a-chord-tone" technique is common to the language of jazz improvisation and can be traced back to Baroque music.

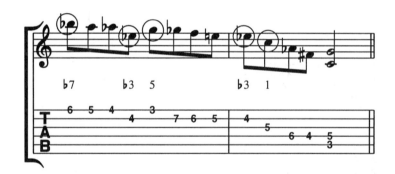

Example 25 (CD 31)

As in the major chord section, substituting the V7 altered sound over the static I (Cm7) chord is employed here in bar 2. Bar 1 begins as an ascending chromatic idea with four notes played under a slur.

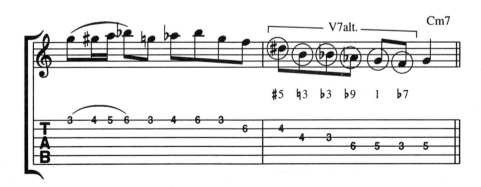

Example 26 (CD 32)

The purpose of this line is to once again illustrate how a phrase can be lengthened by repeating a group of notes through two octaves or more.

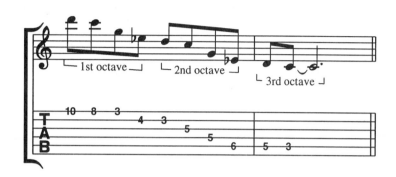

Example 27 (CD 33)

Here again is the same principle of phrase extension through octave repetition, this time via an ascending Cm9 arpeggio.

Example 28 (CD 34)

Next is a descending line that includes all notes from natural minor except the b6 (Ab). This one covers a full three-octave range.

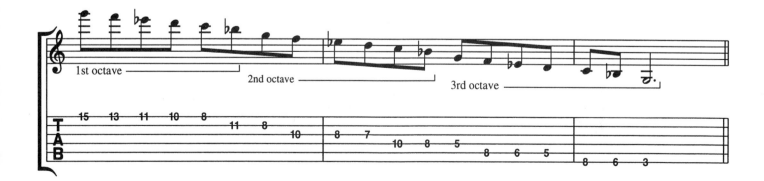

Example 29 (CD 35)

This pattern is a stand-alone line that is not harmonically related to the other examples. Its construction is based on a four-note idea where each successive four-note group is a major 3rd away from the last note in the group. This symmetrical occurrence takes the line pretty far "outside" before resolving to a C minor chord tone (Eb).

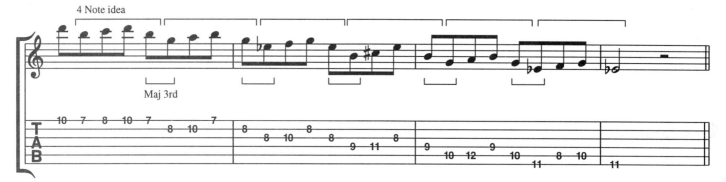

Example 30 (CD 36)

Here we have one continuous line in eighth notes that arcs up and down with a balanced combination of scalewise motion and skips. As usual, study how non-diatonic notes are used in terms of beat placement and resolution.

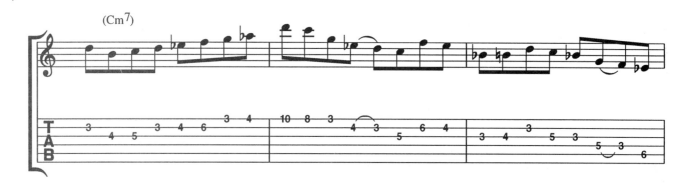

Example 31 (CD 37)

Bar 2 of this example strongly suggests the V7 altered sound before it resolves to Cm in bar 3. See bracket and interval analysis below.

Superimposing Major Triads Over Minor

The concept of superimposing one sound over another can be perceived of in two ways - from a theoretical point of view, involving modes and polychords, or guitaristically, by visualizing and playing shapes on the fingerboard that we know sound good - without asking why. We will focus on the less analytical, more guitaristic approach. Observe the basic chord forms you hold and by rearranging or inverting them across the neck, discover their "puzzles," because when playing lines, the notes you are looking for will be found inside those forms. Thinking of these triad shapes as their own entities will free you from thinking about "what modes/scales work over Cm" - instead you can stay focused on Cm itself.

Example 32 (CD 38)

Here are Bb (Bb D F) and Eb (Eb G Bb) triads for the purpose of superimposing over Cm7.

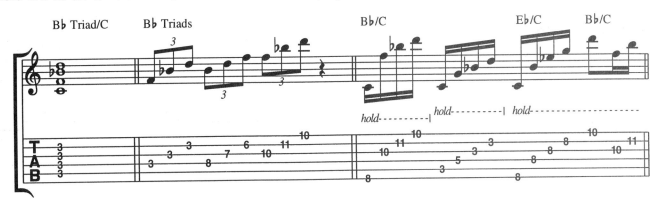

(Example 32 continued)

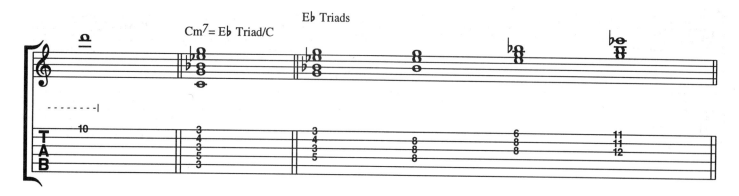

Example 33: Minor Etude (CD 39)

This is a very succinct improvisation over a Cm7 to G7alt vamp that is as "easy to hear" as it is to analyze. As with the "Major Etude", look to the annotations for study assistance.

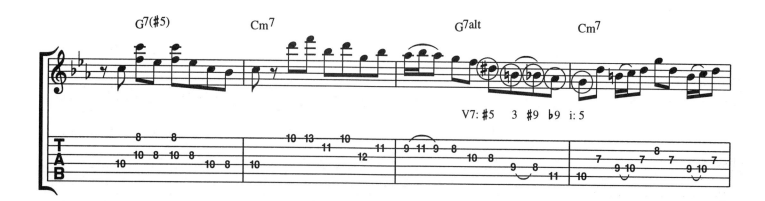

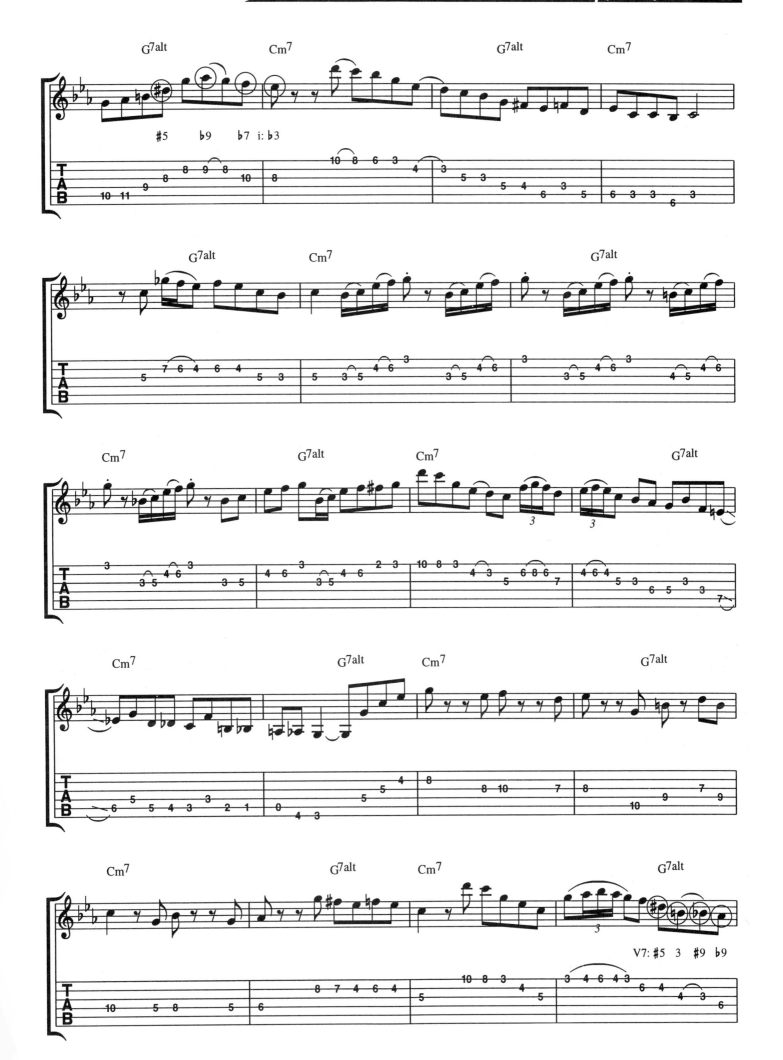

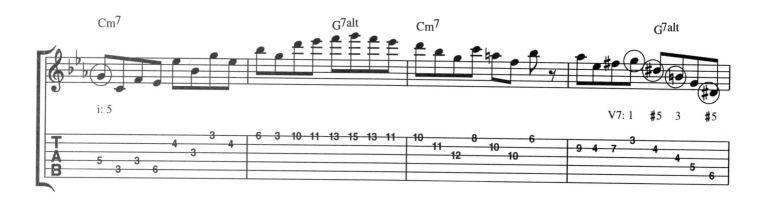

Harmonic Families: Dominant 7

The Dominant 7th chord is the most crucial chord in all music. Jazz has traditionally heightened this chord's importance by exploiting its every shade of color and by inventing infinite ways of working it into chord progressions that if done in Pop or many other styles, would sound outlandish and unacceptable. Before exploring the colors of the altered dominant chord, let us first deal with the static (unresolving) dominant chord. In this case, G7 is used. Because it does not resolve to some type of C chord, there is no need to motivate it towards resolution by adding tensions.

Example 34 (CD 40)

The "G7 sound" is exemplified by this 3rd position voicing of a G13 chord, which is simply G7 (G B D F) with the added 13 (E). The scale that is used is G mixolydian (G A B C D E F) and it can be considered to be the "complete sound" of G13. For the purpose of analysis, any note outside of the scale can be thought of as non-diatonic.

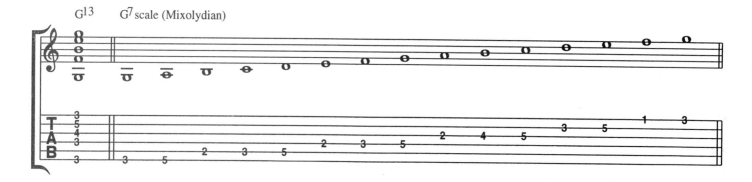

Example 35 (CD 41)

This line is similar to other descending lines we have been hearing, only it uniquely begins from the 13th (E) and extends beyond three octaves and finally resolves on the 3rd (B).

Example 36 (CD 42)

This is a purely diatonic, rising-and-falling idea that combines the intervals of 3rds and 2nds.

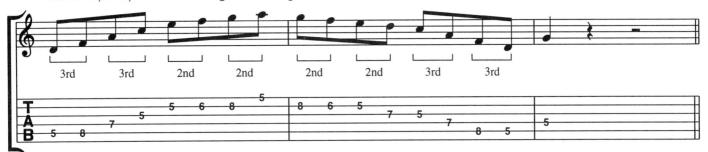

Example 37 (CD 43)

Here are a collection of phrases that outline the G7 sound with many twists and turns. Notice the consistent eighth note rhythm and balanced, arcing shape of the lines. Non-diatonic notes in this example are used as passing tones as opposed to altered dominant implications - which is the next subject.

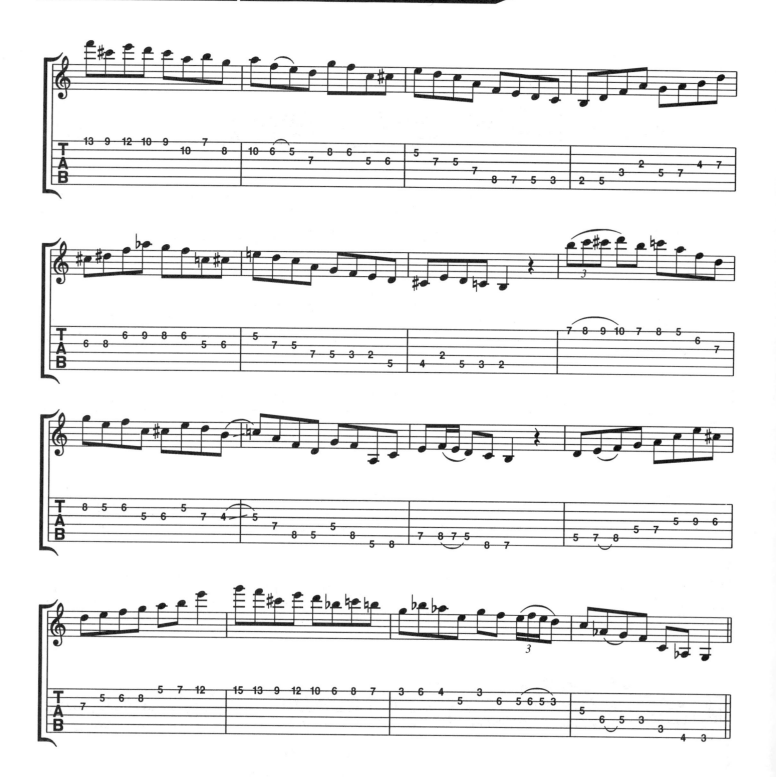

Example 38: Static Dominant Etude (CD 44)

This next improvisation completely explores the sound of the G7 chord. The majority of the solo makes use of G Mixolydian exclusively, with chromatic passing tones and other non-diatonic notes for occasional color - see circled interval identifications. Many neck positions are covered throughout, and it would be useful to memorize phrases that you are attracted to, both in terms of their fingerings and intervallic relationship to the chord - specifically for the purpose of transposition. These ideas should not begin and end only for a G7 chord; bring what you will to other dominant 7th chords in other keys.

Example 38:

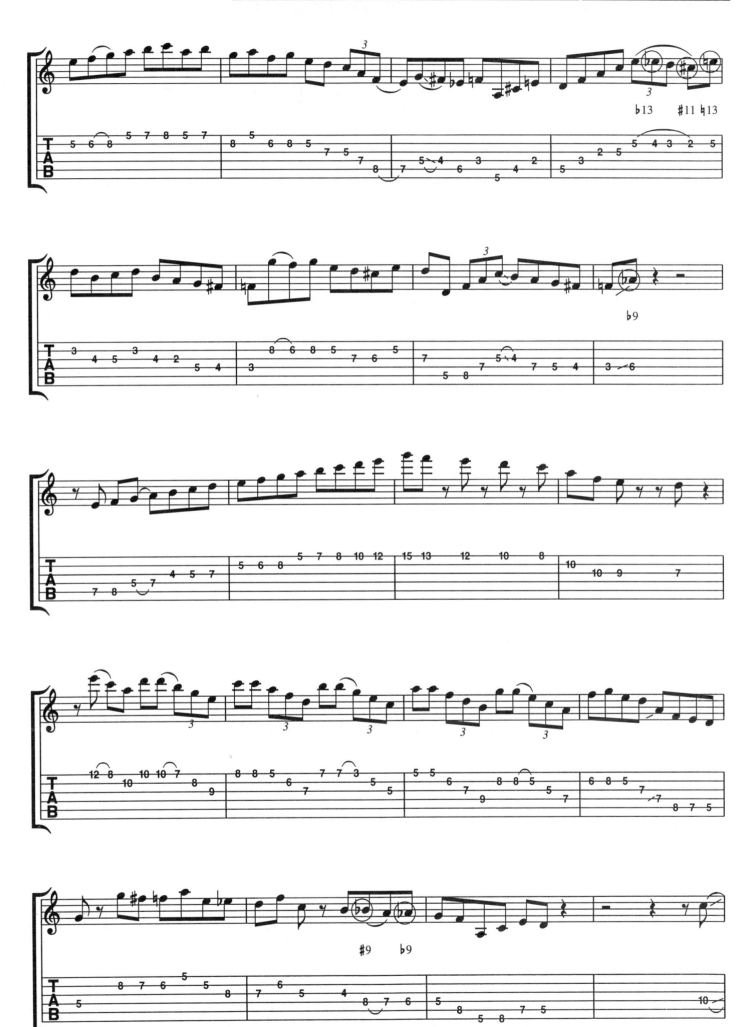

Altered Dominant Lines

In jazz, "altered" refers to a specific group of notes or tensions that when placed on a dominant 7th chord create a very strong motivation towards resolution. The tensions are the b5/#5 and b9/#9. These four possibilities are often found in numerous combinations. When the altered dominant chord is involved, it is necessary to alter our lines to fit that chord. While the unaltered dominant chord calls for the mixolydian scale, the altered dominant has the "altered scale." Let's check out a few chord voicings for the altered dominant sound.

Example 39 (CD 45)

Each of these voicings include the low G root on the 6th string - which is certainly not necessary to the effect of the chord. They are included here due to the "solo guitar" situation. When playing with a bassist or keyboard player, you may want to leave out the roots in order to allow yourself more maneuverability. The chords are analyzed here in terms of chord-tones and tensions present.

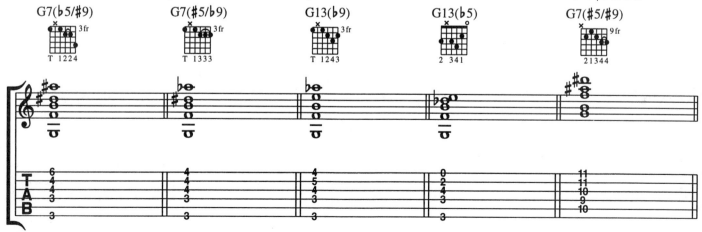

Example 40 (CD 46)

Here is a two-octave altered scale. Notice that whenever possible, the ♯3 and ♭7 are held to emphasize the "complete altered dominant sound." It is very important to recognize each and every degree of the altered scale in respect to its relationship to the root of the dominant chord. In this case, the low root is found on the 3rd fret, 6th string. When working the altered scale out in other positions, recognize the lowest root possible and relate all scale degrees against it. See the 8th position version of the G altered scale as an example.

G altered scale (2nd position)   G altered scale (8th position)

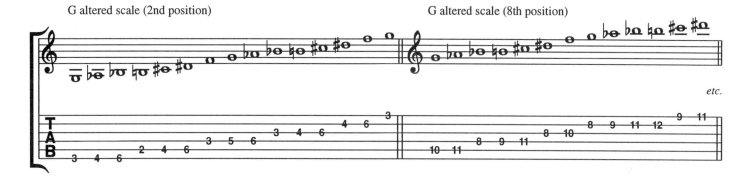

Example 41 (CD 47)

This example serves as a perfect working model of strong altered scale lines limited to 3rd position. It would be helpful to transpose this example to other keys by simply moving it up to a higher fret. Always keep track of the intervals in relation to the root.

Example 42 (CD 48)

These three lines are related in an interesting way. Each one is in a different position and starts on different chord tones; however, their shape and fingerings are similar.

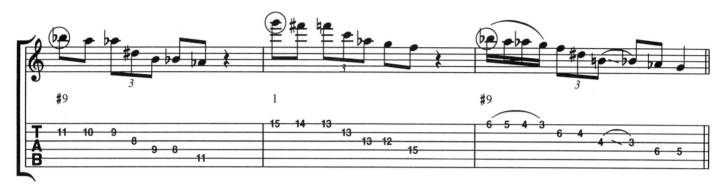

The Diminished Scale For Altered Dominant Chords

Example 43

Earlier we worked with the diminished chord "shape" superimposed over a dominant 7th chord. What we are about to do takes this concept a step further, as we superimpose the entire diminished scale over the altered dominant chord. It should be understood that the diminished scale is an eight-note symmetrical organization of whole steps and half steps.

Diminished whole/half step: **W H W H W H W**

Diminished half/whole step: **H W H W H W H**

For this study, we will deal with the half/whole sequence starting on G.

	H	**W**	**H**	**W**	**H**	**W**	**H**
G	Ab	Bb	B	C#	D	E	F
1	b2	b3	3	#4	5	6	b7
	b9	#9		#11		13	

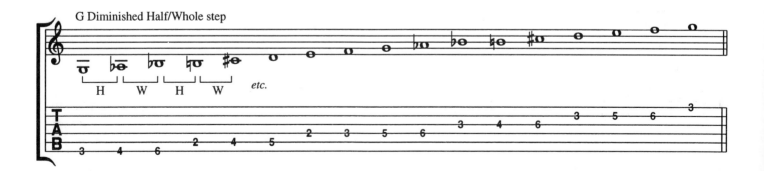

Example 44 (CD 49)

Compared to the altered scale, it's clear that the first five scale degrees are identical, while the remainder have important differences: The diminished scale has a ♮5 and ♮6 that the altered scale does not have. The common degrees are 1 ♭2 ♭3 ♯3 ♯4 and ♭7. Because of the ♮6 (or ♮13) especially, this scale would be a better choice for dominant chords that have the ♭9/13 combination - like the 3rd chord in Example 39. Its symmetrical design allows for infinite pattern possibilities that have long been part of the jazz vernacular, dating back to the Bebop period. The following are based on the G diminished half/whole step scale.

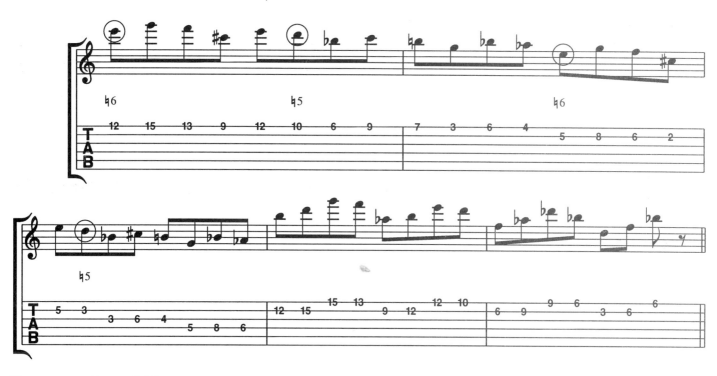

Example 45 (CD 50)

Here are G diminished half/whole step scale ideas running through all six strings. The first two bars of this G diminished phrase are found in the form of a useful arpeggio. The final three bars are again inspired by Bebop patterns.

The Tri-Tone Substitution
For Altered Dominant Chords

In the same manner that we superimposed major triads over minor chords, a similar concept applies here with regard to the altered dominant chord. The tri-tone substitution is achieved by building a dominant 7th chord from the lowered 5th degree of the dominant chord in question. A tri-tone is an interval of a diminished fifth (three whole steps). The tri-tone above G is Db, the lowered 5th.

Placing a Db7 chord (Db F Ab Cb) over the G7 altered chord creates a sound that is very much a part of the jazz language. Once you can recognize the Db7 shapes over a G7 chord, you will begin to expand beyond shapes, playing lines found within them. Notice which intervals occur when comparing Db7 against G7:

G7:	G	B	D	F	A	B
	1	3	5	b7	9	
			b5	b7	b9	3
Db7:			Db	F	Ab	Cb (B)

Notice that the 3rd and 7th of G7 (the two most important notes of a dominant 7th chord) are also contained within the Db7 (reversed as the 7th and 3rd). The chord frames show the common tones between G7 and Db7.

Example 46 (CD 51)

Here the Db7 can be found in this line that extends up to 7th position as it reaches for the high Db in bar 2. See circled notations for Db7 notes.

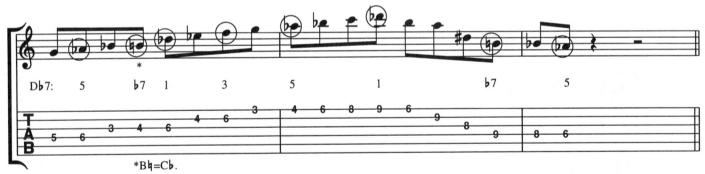

*B♮=Cb.

Example 47 (CD 52)

One last example that again melds Db7, G altered scale and G diminished scale ideas together in two tasteful, balanced phrases.

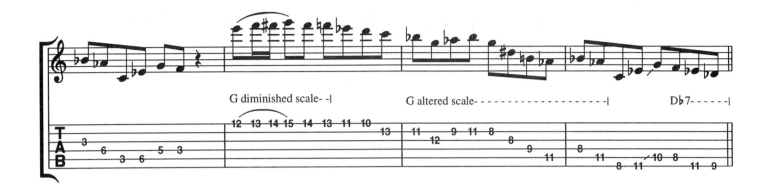

Example 48: *Turnaround Etude* (CD 53)

The I vi ii V chord progression is the foundation of many jazz chord progressions and is often used as a means to "turn the phrase around" and begin anew. In this etude, we are going to study how to connect these chords as they constantly repeat in a loop. Although examining how each line relates to each chord can be advantageous, it may be best to "look at the big picture" and consider how the ii chord (Dm7) - and for all intents and purposes, the vi chord as well are lumped into one big V chord (G7). In the big picture, the material we have been working with concerning the V chord can be heard starting at the Am7, all the way through to the resolution at the I chord. Analyze all notes with accidentals as usual: chord-tone/non-chord-tone, beat placement of tensions and resolutions, arpeggios, patterns, superimpositions, etc.

The "cadenza" section at the end is made up of arpeggios that are clearly laying out the chords they represent. The final resolution to Cmaj7 is extended by adding Ab13/#11: an altered dominant a halfstep above the V, Db9/#11, another altered dominant substituting for the expected Dm7, and finally a ii-V (Dm7b5 - G7 altered) to Cmaj7.

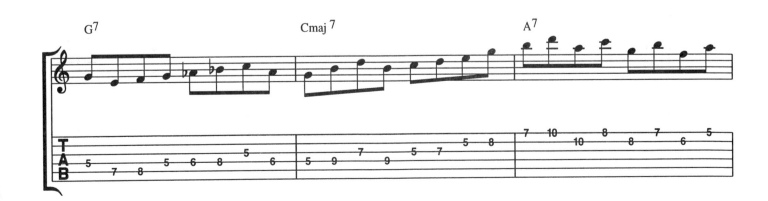

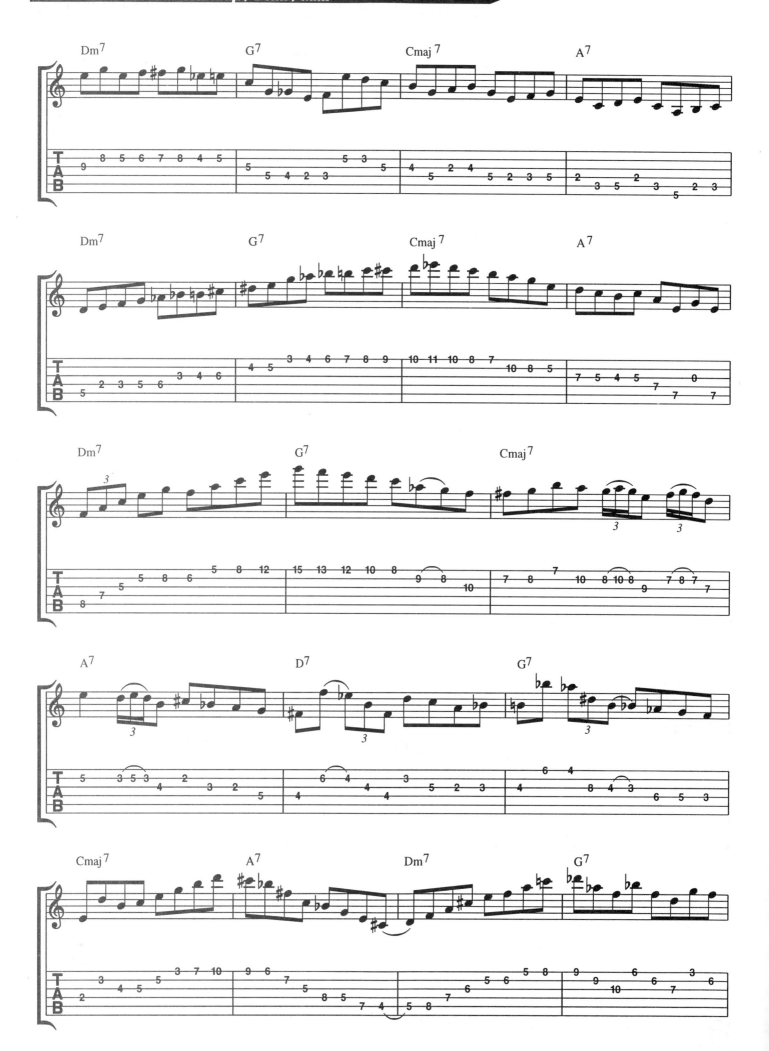

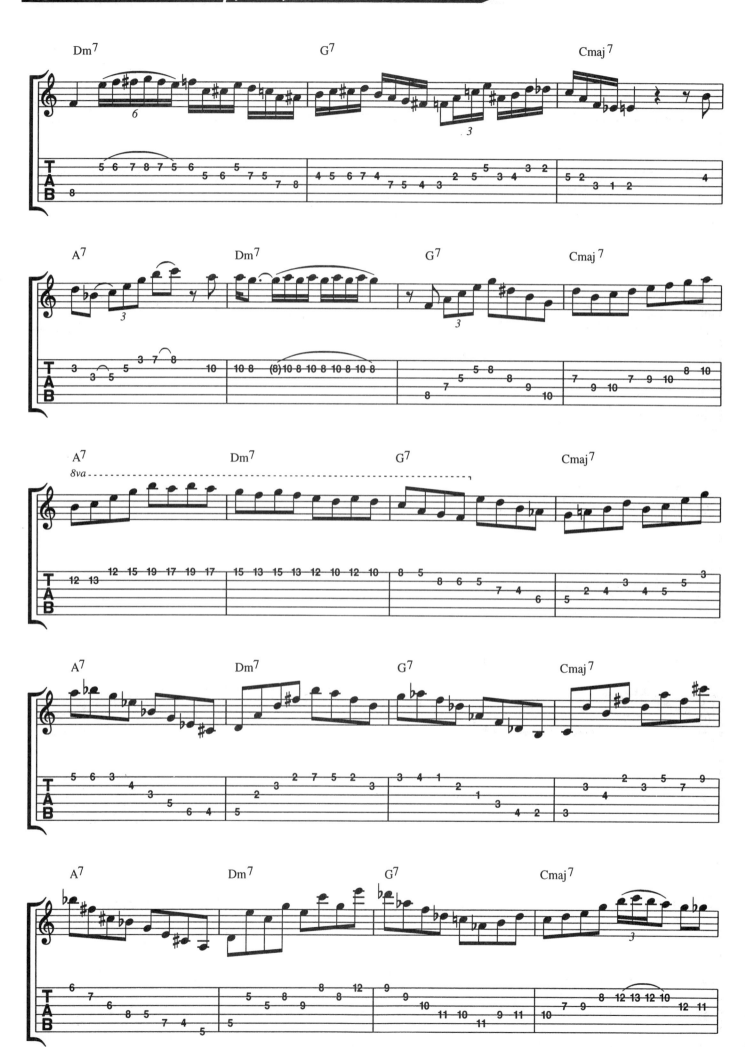

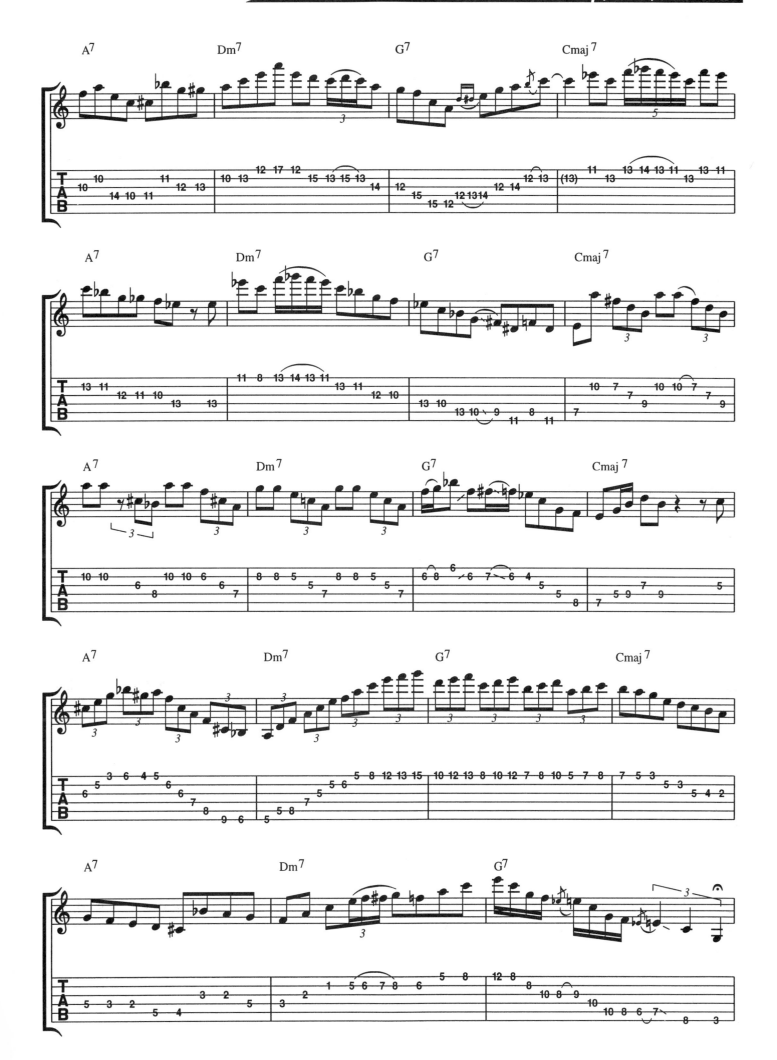

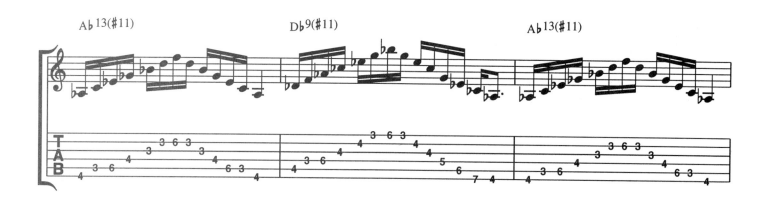

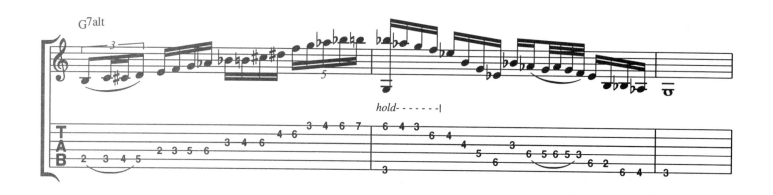

Scales For Altered Dominant Turnarounds

Example 49 (CD 54)

These are "sample" fingerings for the following altered dominant chords:

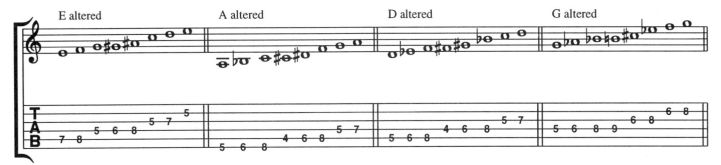

Example 50: Altered Dominant Turnaround Etude (CD 55)

The turnaround we will be working with here is related to the I vi ii V of the last example. However, in this case, all of the chords are altered dominant types and the I chord is replaced by a III (E7#9/#11) chord. Each chord employs the altered scale from their respective roots: E altered, D altered and G altered.

A few observations concerning this example:

    1. The harmonic content of the lines adheres rather strictly to the scales as shown in Example 49, so analyzing them should be easy.

    2. Unlike the prior turnaround etude (I vi ii V), chords are approached on an individual basis, with a clear-cut scale-per-chord relationship. Chords are never "lumped together," which makes connecting them more challenging.

    3. The rhythm of these lines is varied and decidedly freer than all other examples thus far. There exists a good amount of "double-time" - playing sixteenth notes instead of the usual eighths - thereby packing more tensions per beat.

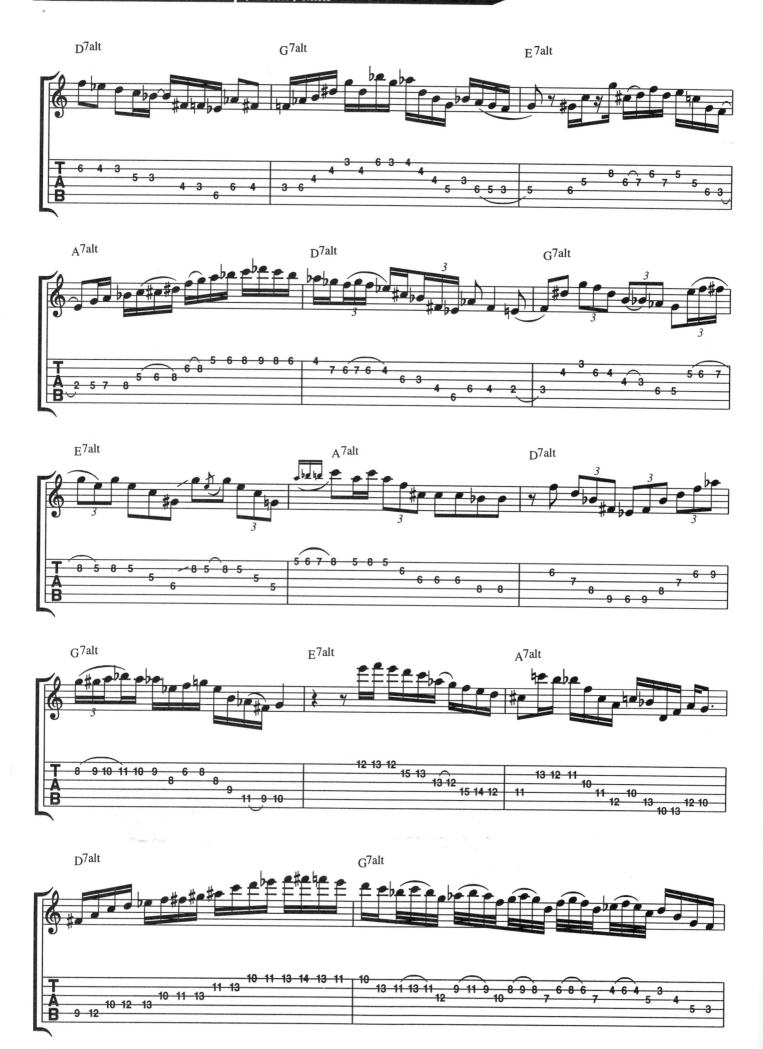

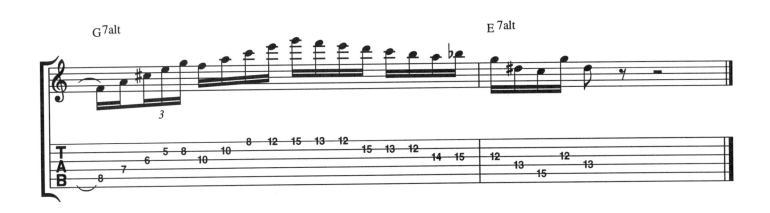

Performance Section

Concerning Chord-Melody Style

1. Generally, it is best to keep the melody on the top three strings. This way, your harmonization beneath allows access to more strings in an appropriate range of the instrument. Voicing the melody of a song lower than the G (3rd string) will force you to place chord tones above the melody - which will tend to obscure and lessen its strength and importance. Playing a melody in a middle-to-low register of the guitar tends not to "speak" as well.

2. The process of harmonizing a melody with chords can be thought of as "adding color." Once you know what family (Major, Minor, Dominant) you are using to harmonize with, add whatever degree of color you hear at a given moment. As the colors become bolder, the more you depart from the expected. Rather than thinking of this departure as "re-harmonization," try approaching it as a colorful harmonization.

3. Because melody alone very often implies chords, it is not necessary to go to great pains and work very hard to accompany every melody note with a chord. There is no sense in "killing yourself for no reason." Even a very rhythmically short chord can stay in the listener's ear until the next harmonic change arises. You may choose to play more chords per bar for certain reasons, but always be aware that the melody needs to "breathe" and over-harmonizing can suffocate its impact.

4. Adding "voice movement" to your chords will add impetus and interest to your music. What "voice movement" refers to is when one or more chord tones move - usually by steps, diatonic or chromatic - to resolving chord tones in the next chord. This can occur while the melody and stationary chord tones are also sounding, or in between them as "filler." When employed well, it can give the illusion of a great deal more going on than there actually is.

5. "Grips" (chord forms) tend to dictate melody, and the most natural reaction to improvising chord-melody style is to simplify the infinite possibilities and play only what you hear and what falls right in the vicinity of the grip. "What you are looking for is right around your fingers."

6. Remember: "The object of chord-melody is to make music, not hard work; you play the guitar, not the other way around."

All The Things You Are

Lyrics by OSCAR HAMMERSTEIN II
Music by JEROME KERN

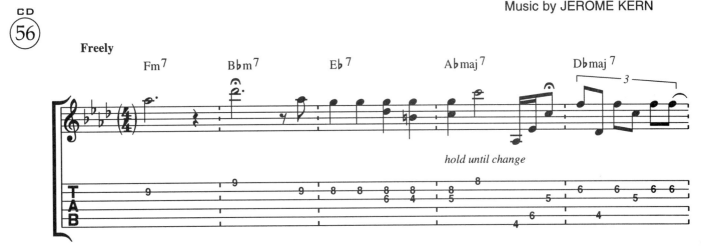

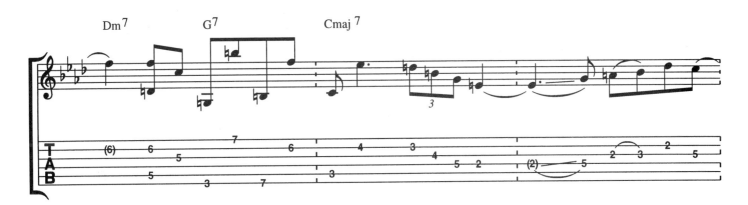

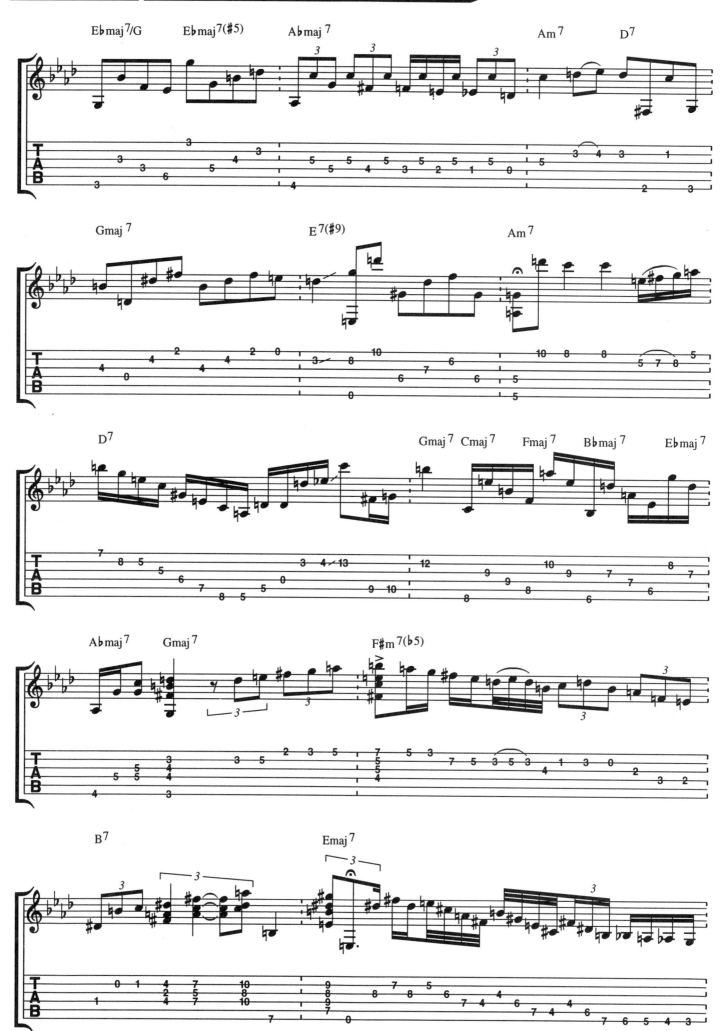

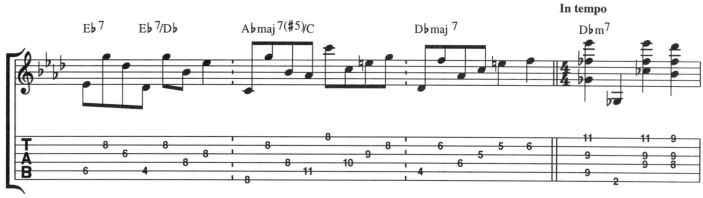

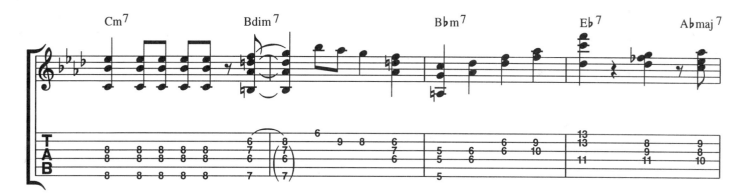

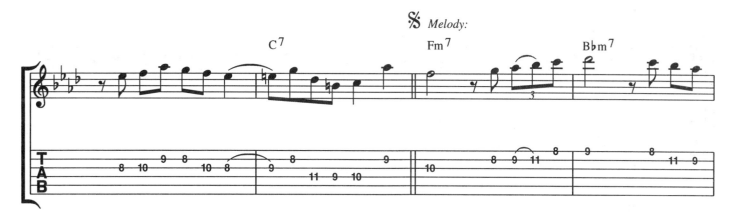

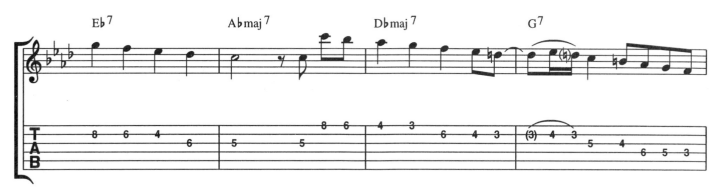

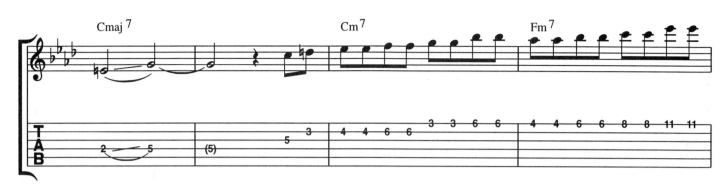

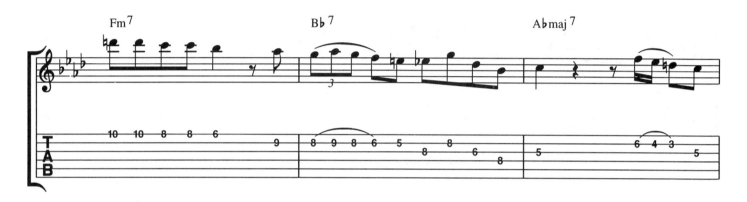

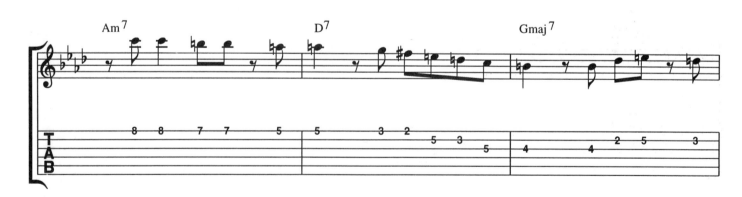

*Ab sounds at pull-off.

*Hammer-on string w/ out picking.

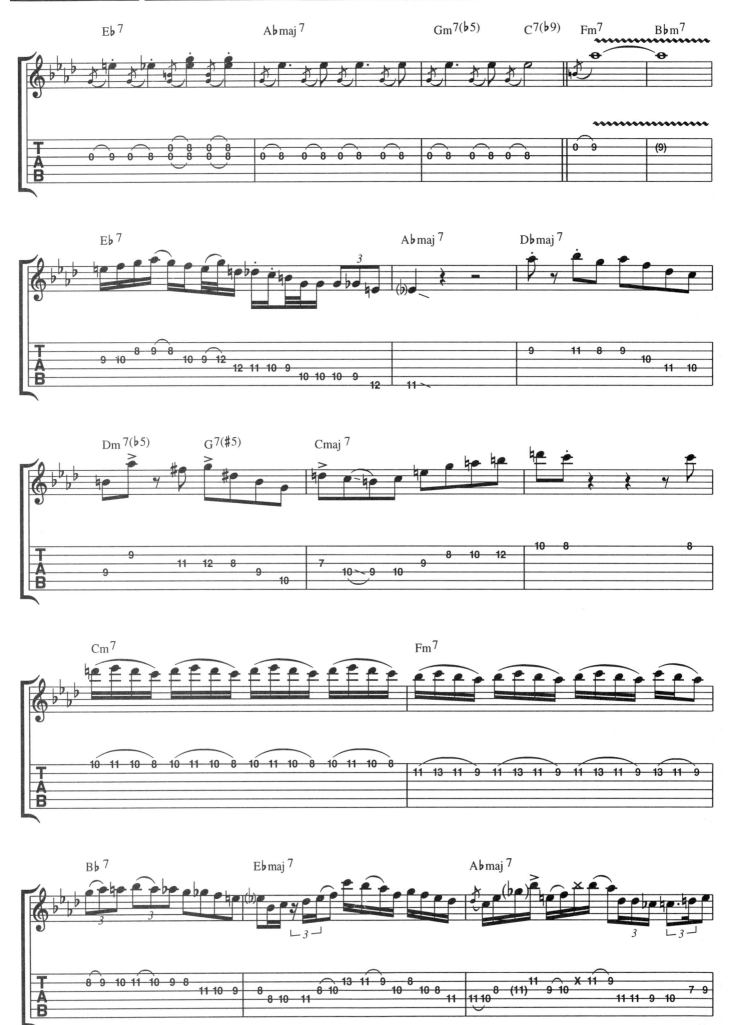

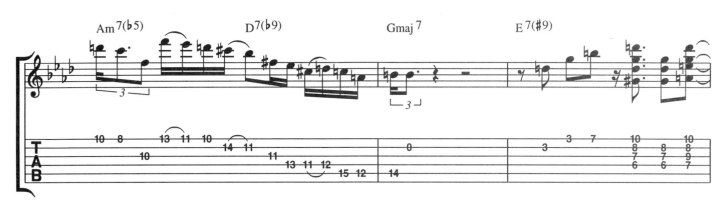

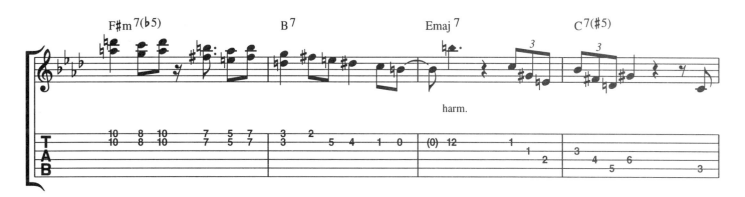

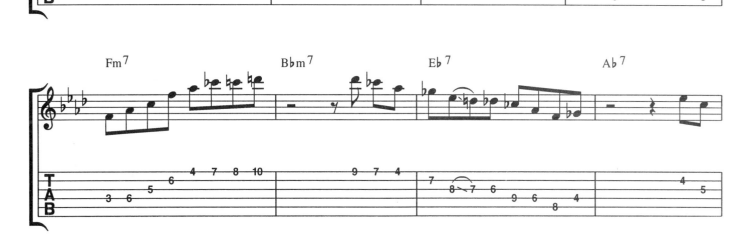

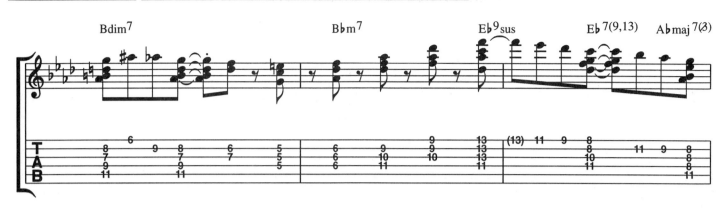

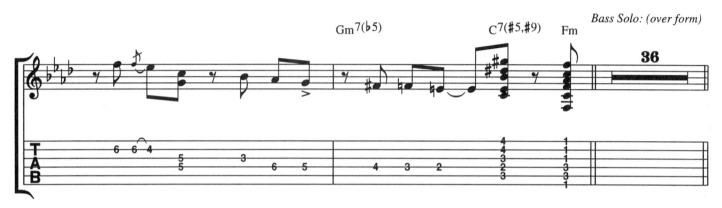

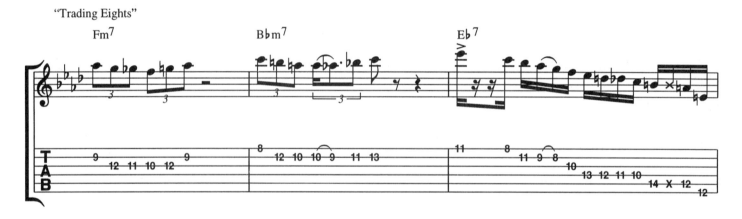

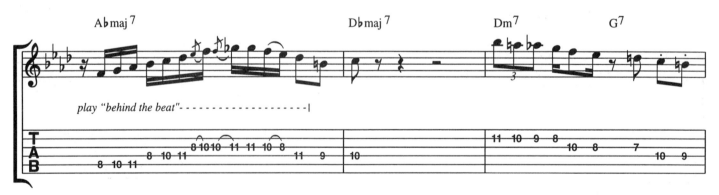

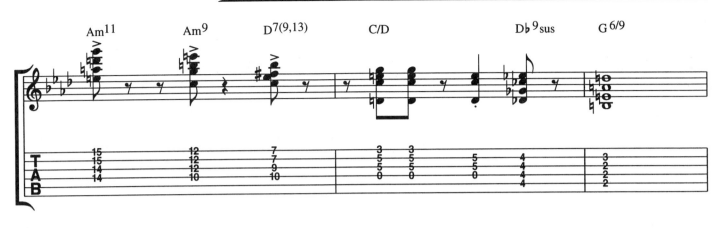

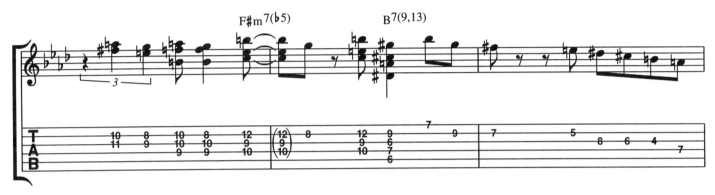

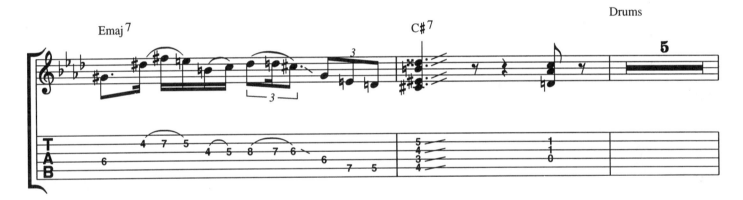

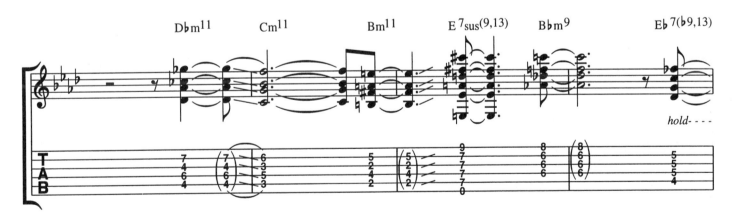

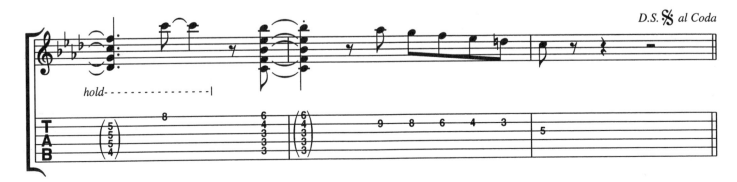

Joe's Blues

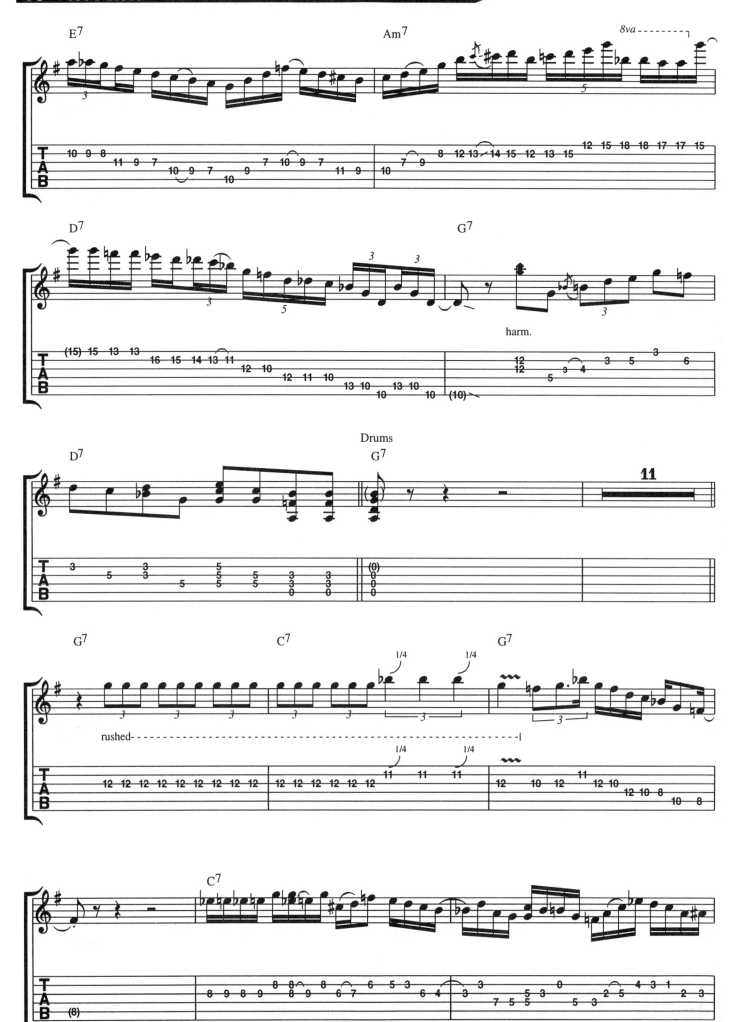

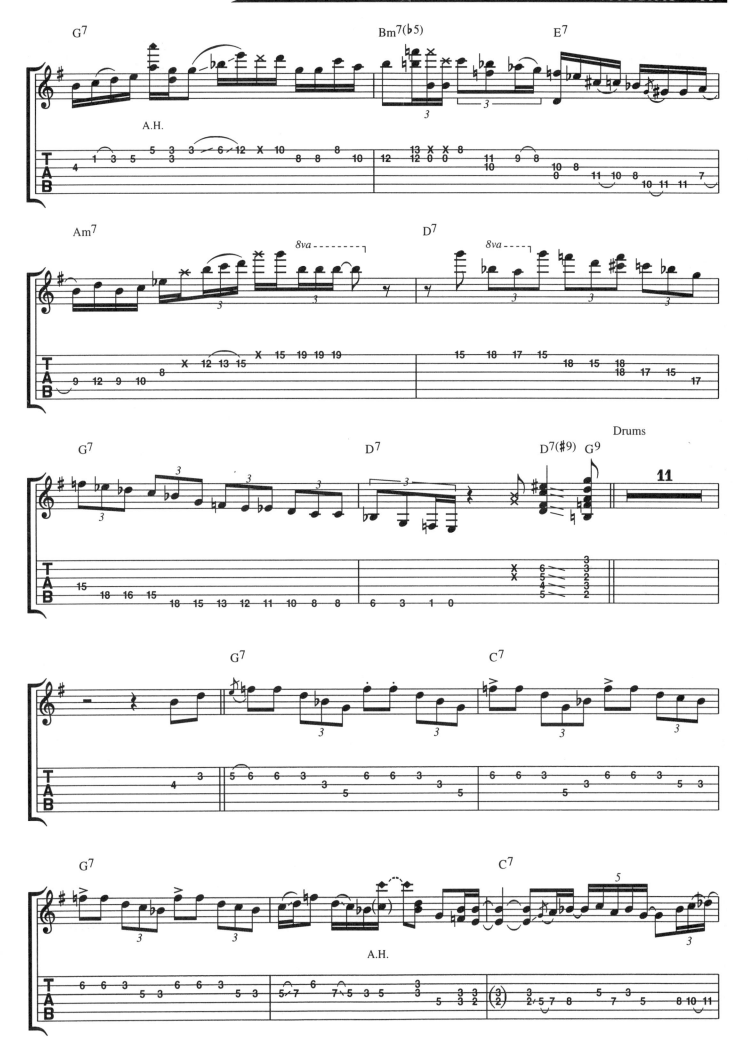

Freely

*Hammer-on to string without picking.

†Pop w/ thumb.

Stella By Starlight

Lyrics by NED WASHINGTON
Music by VICTOR YOUNG

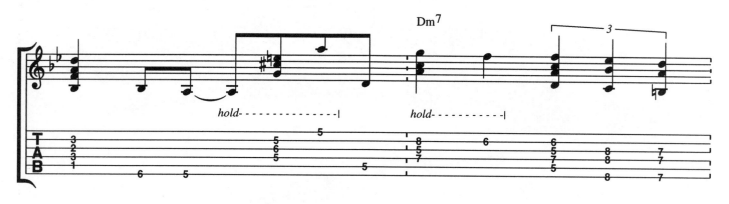

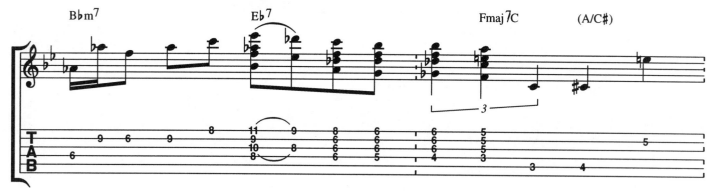

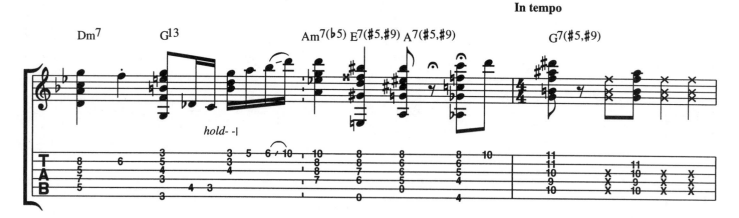

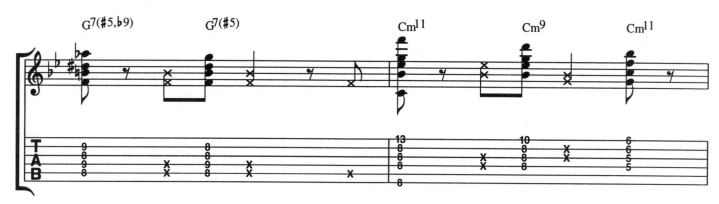

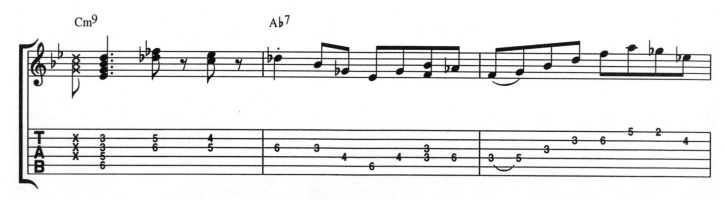

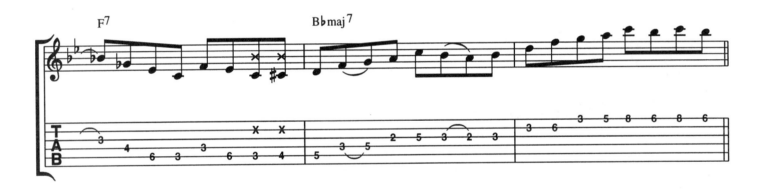

*D sounds at pull-off.

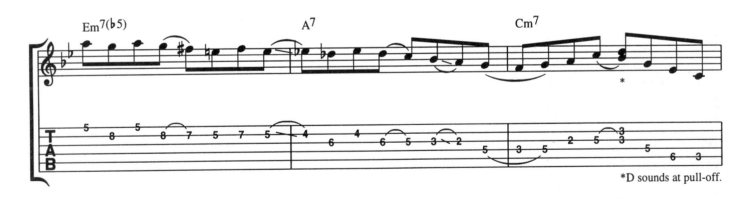

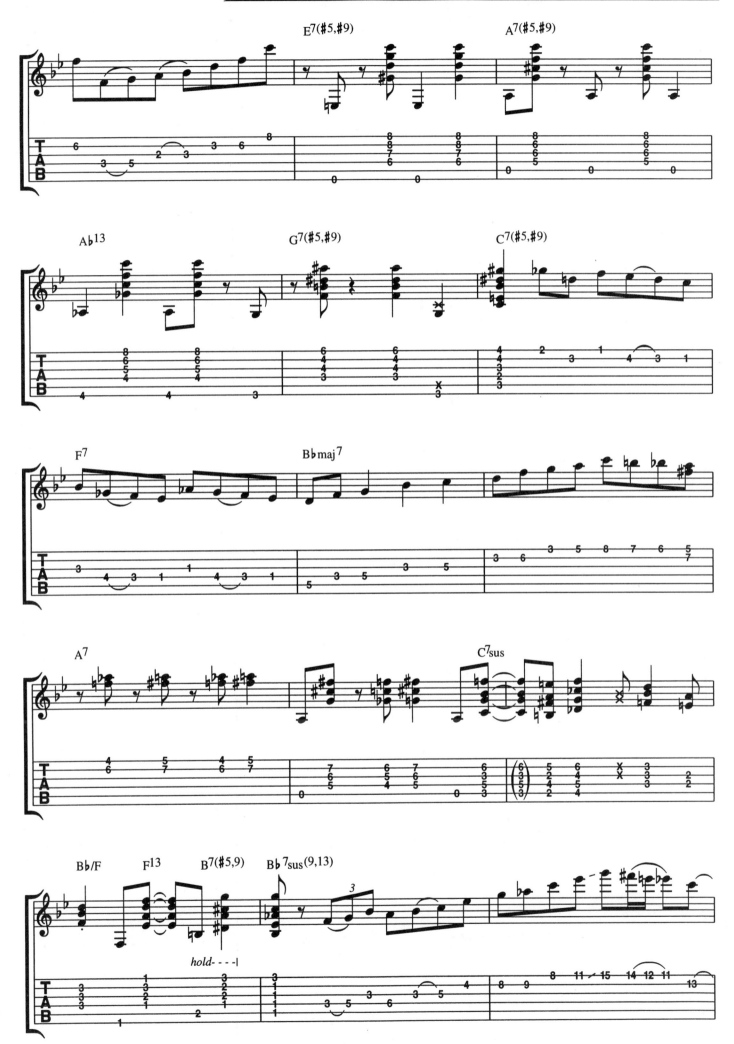

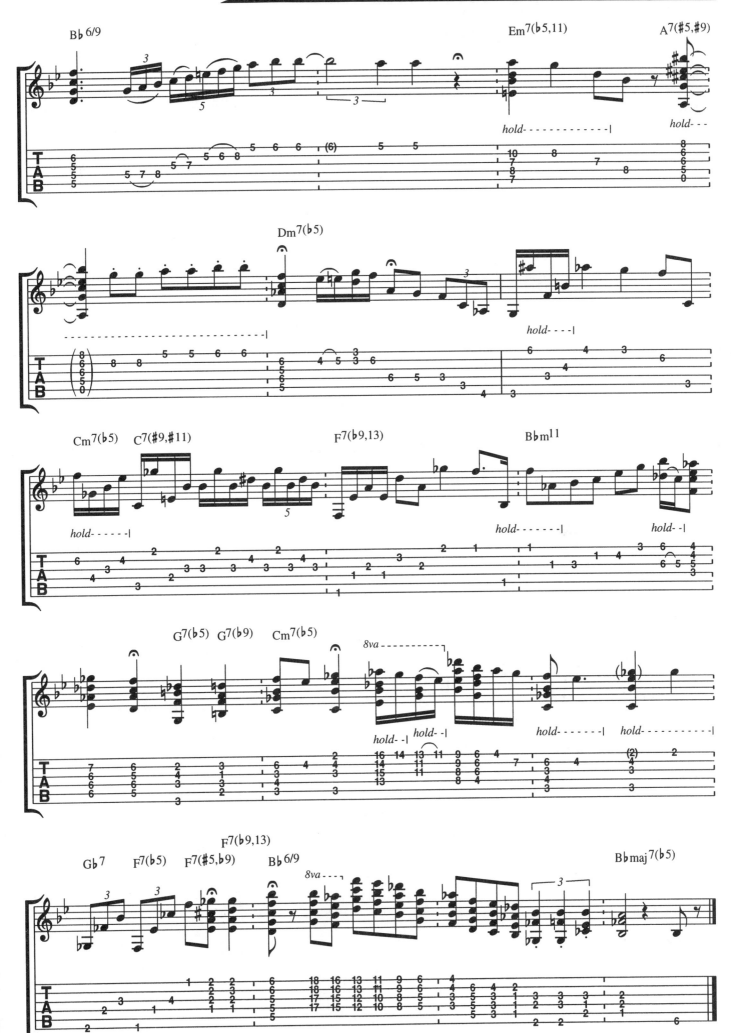

GUITAR TAB GLOSSARY **

TABLATURE EXPLANATION

READING TABLATURE: Tablature illustrates the six strings of the guitar. Notes and chords are indicated by the placement of fret numbers on a given string(s).

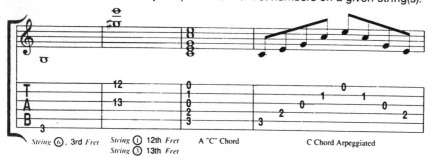

String ⑥, 3rd *Fret*   String ① 12th *Fret*   A "C" Chord   C Chord Arpeggiated
String ③ 13th *Fret*

BENDING NOTES

HALF STEP: Play the note and bend string one half step.*

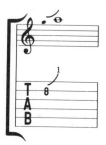

WHOLE STEP: Play the note and bend string one whole step.

PREBEND AND RELEASE: Bend the string, play it, then release to the original note.

RHYTHM SLASHES

STRUM INDICATIONS: Strum with indicated rhythm.

The chord voicings are found on the first page of the transcription underneath the song title.

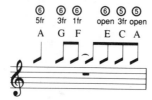

INDICATING SINGLE NOTES USING RHYTHM SLASHES: Very often single notes are incorporated into a rhythm part. The note name is indicated above the rhythm slash with a fret number and a string indication.

*A half step is the smallest interval in Western music; it is equal to one fret. A whole step equals two frets.

**By Kenn Chipkin and Aaron Stang

ARTICULATIONS

HAMMER ON: Play lower note, then "hammer on" to higher note with another finger. Only the first note is attacked.

PULL OFF: Play higher note, then "pull off" to lower note with another finger. Only the first note is attacked.

LEGATO SLIDE: Play note and slide to the following note. (Only first note is attacked).

PALM MUTE: The note or notes are muted by the palm of the pick hand by lightly touching the string(s) near the bridge.

ACCENT: Notes or chords are to be played with added emphasis.

DOWN STROKES AND UPSTROKES: Notes or chords are to be played with either a downstroke (⊓ ·) or upstroke (∨) of the pick.